I am a Strong Woman of God

Dear beautiful, strong, unique woman of God.

I made this book to combine coloring and creativity with devotion to the Lord. It features powerful Bible verses that are particularly relevant to women today.

The coloring pages are single-sided to prevent bleed through to the next coloring page. The left-hand pages are used to give the Bible quote in full to help explain the passage better and locate where it appears in the Bible.

I sincerely hope this coloring book gives you as much joy, peace and inspiration as it gave me in creating it.

Wishing you love and blessings,

PS. I would be very grateful if you could kindly leave a review on Amazon.

'God is in the midst of her, she shall not be moved. God shall help her'

Psalms 46:5

'Even so their wives must be grave, not slanderers, sober, faithful in all things'

Timothy 3:11

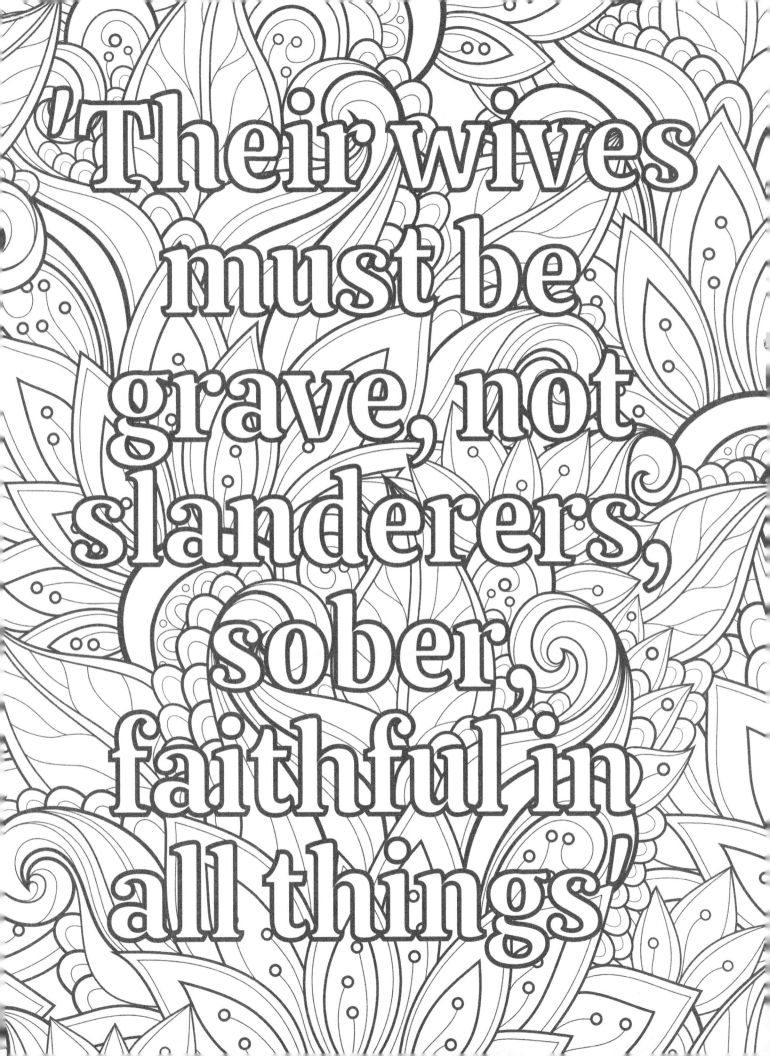

'Their wives must be grave, not slanderers, sober, faithful in all things'

'And blessed is she that believed: for there shall be a performance of those things which were told her from the Lord'

Luke 1:45

'Favour is deceitful, and beauty is vain: but a woman that feareth the Lord, she shall be praised. Give her of the fruit of her hands and let her own works praise her in the gates'

Proverbs 31:30-33

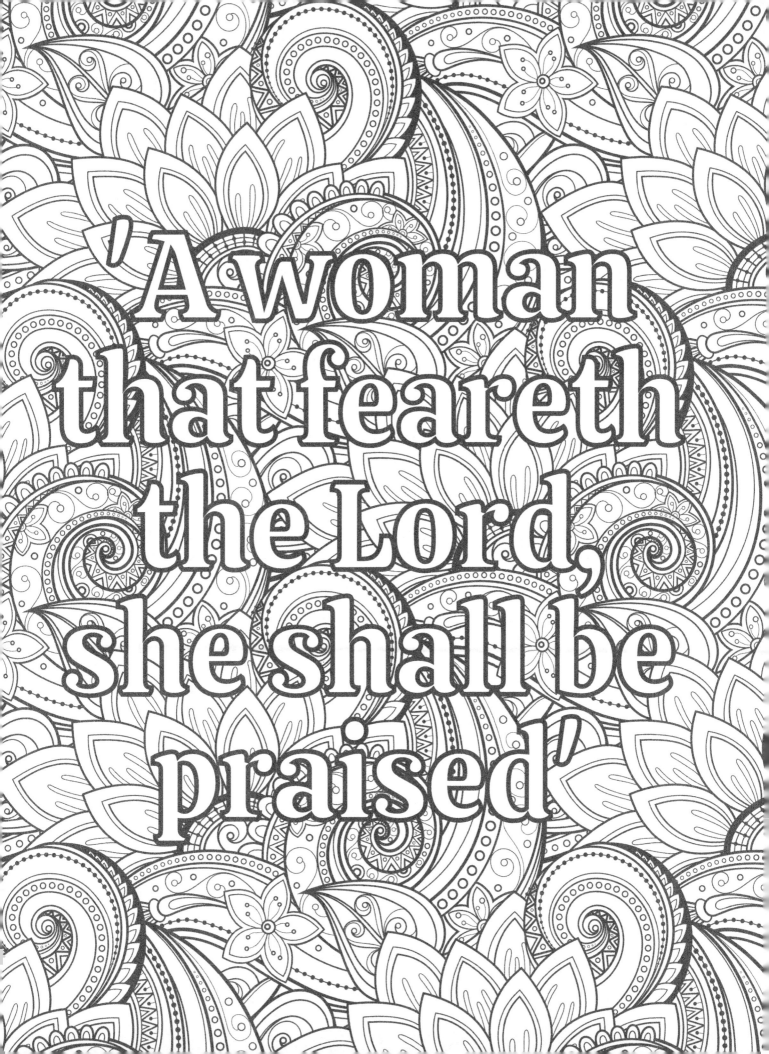

'She considereth a field, and buyeth it: with the fruit of her hands she planteth a vineyard. She girdeth her loins with strength, and strengtheneth her arms'

Proverbs 31:16

'She stretcheth out her hand to the poor, yea, she reacheth forth her hands to the needy. She is not afraid of the snow for her household: for all her household are clothed with scarlet'

Proverbs 31:20

'I will praise thee; for I am fearfully and wonderfully made: marvellous are thy works; and that my soul knoweth right well'

Psalms 139:14

'Have not I commanded thee? Be strong and of a good courage, be not afraid, neither be thou dismayed: for the Lord thy God is with thee whithersoever thou goest'

Joshua 1:9

'A gracious woman retaineth honour: and strong men retain riches'

Proverbs 11:16

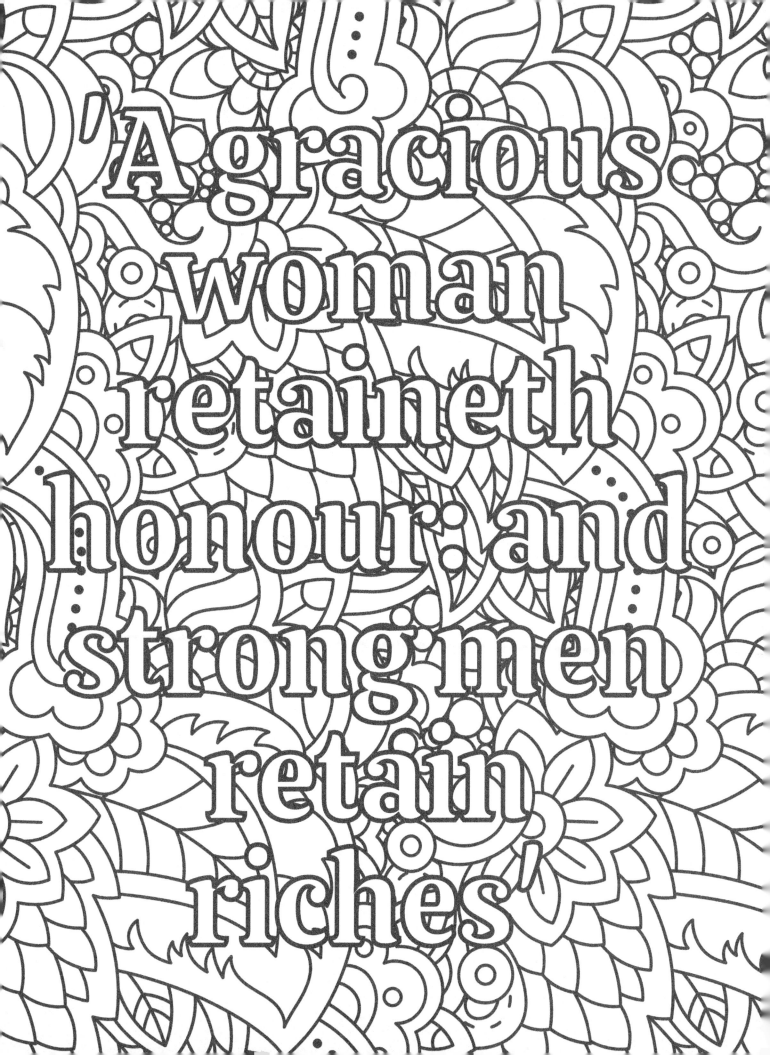

'A gracious woman retaineth honour: and strong men retain riches'

'Strength and honour are her clothing; and she shall rejoice in time to come. With God wrapping us with strength and love, we should not fear for the future'

Proverbs 31:25

'Strength and honour are her clothing'

'She is more precious than rubies: and all the things thou canst desire are not to be compared unto her'

Proverbs 3:15

'She openeth her mouth with wisdom; and in her tongue is the law of kindness'

Proverbs 31:26

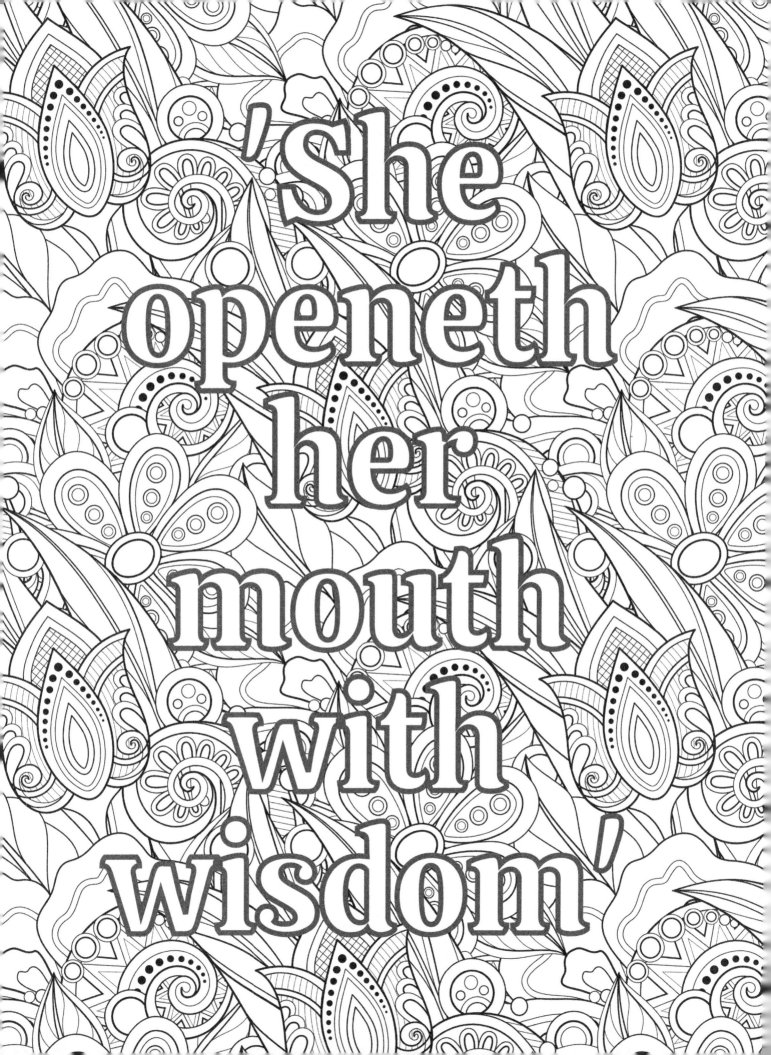

'She openeth her mouth with wisdom'

'Every wise woman buildeth her house: but the foolish plucketh it down with her hands'

Proverbs 14:1

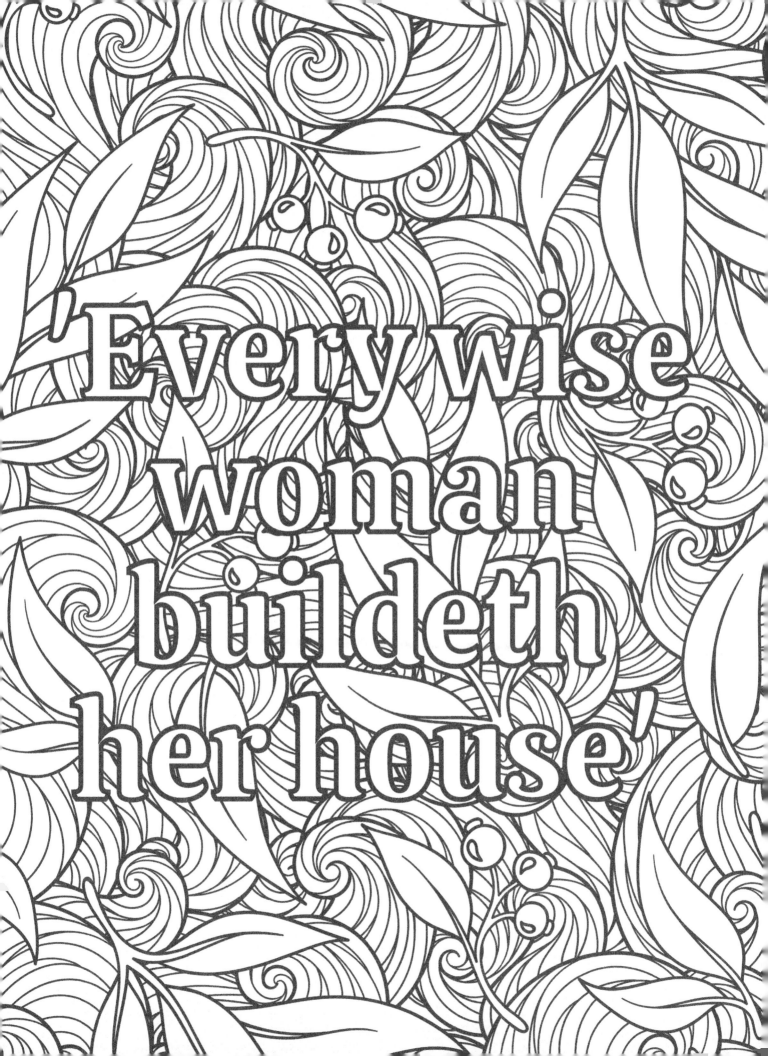

'Every wise woman buildeth her house'

'Whenever you feel unloved, unimportant or insecure, remember to whom you belong'

Ephesians 2:19-22

'The aged women likewise, that they be in behaviour as becometh holiness, not false accusers, not given to much wine, teachers of good things. That they may teach the young women to be sober, to love their husbands, to love their children. To be discreet, chaste, keepers at home, good'

Titus 2:3-5

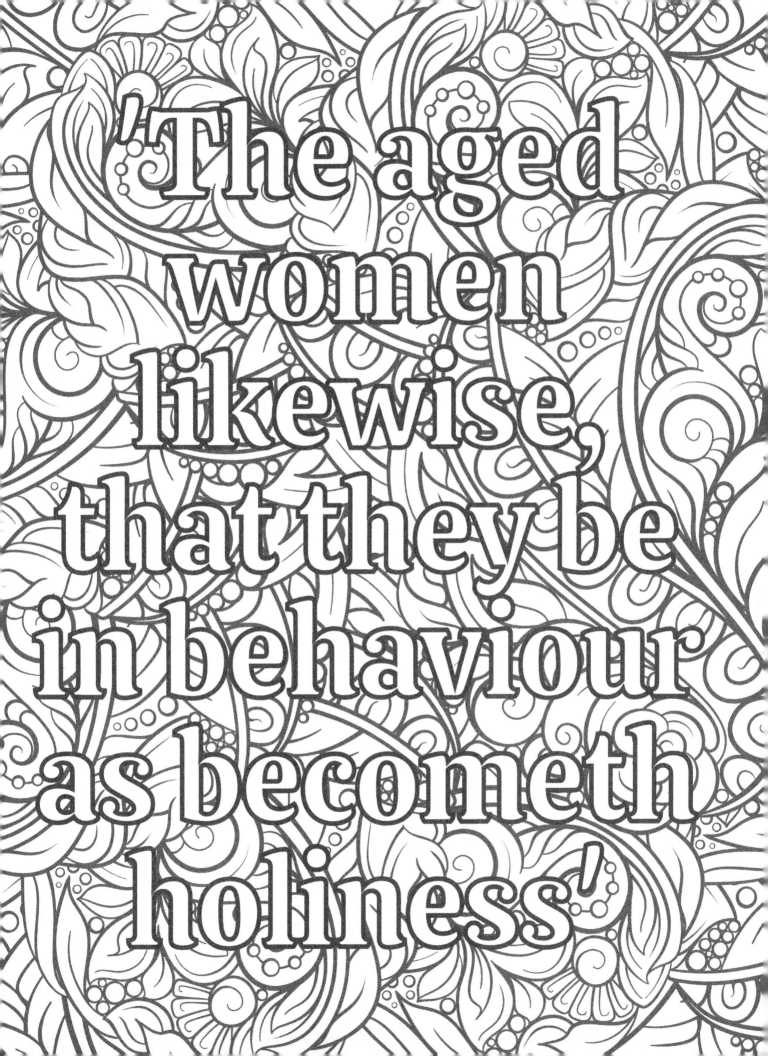

'In like manner also, that women adorn themselves in modest apparel, with shamefacedness and sobriety; not with broided hair, or gold, or pearls, or costly array. But (which becometh women professing godliness) with good works'

Timothy 2:9-10

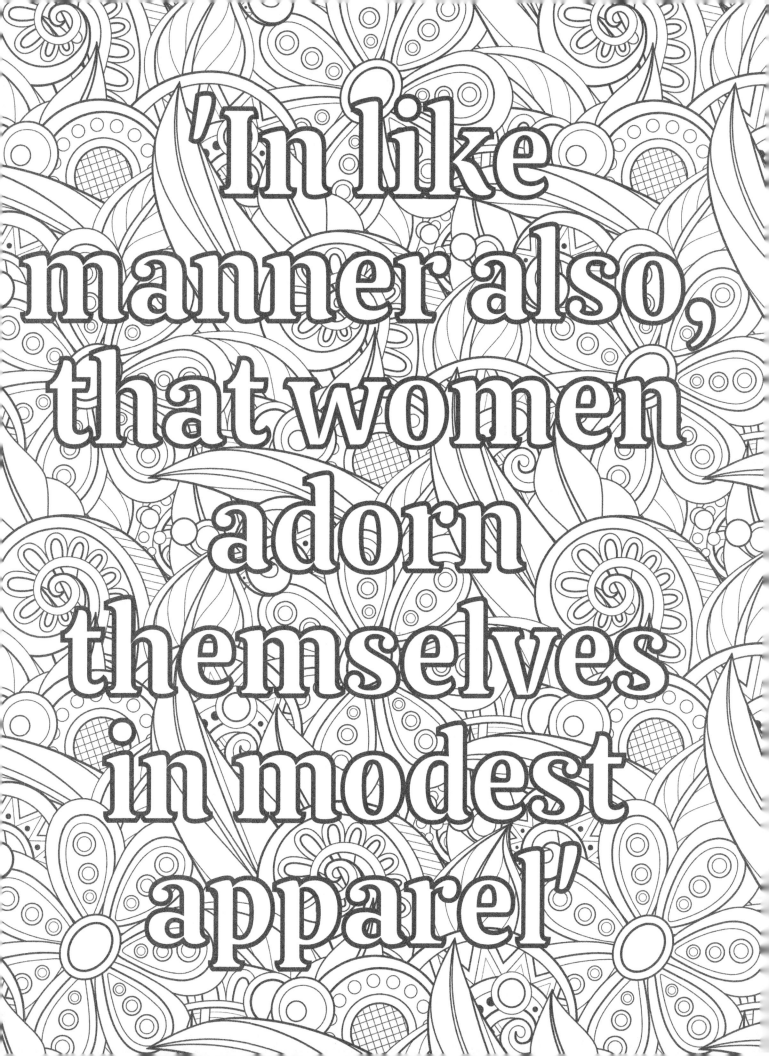

'In like manner also, that women adorn themselves in modest apparel'

'Let the woman learn in silence with all subjection. But I suffer not a woman to teach, nor to usurp authority over the man, but to be in silence. For Adam was first formed, then Eve. And Adam was not deceived, but the woman being deceived was in the transgression. Notwithstanding she shall be saved in childbearing, if they continue in faith and charity and holiness with sobriety'

Timothy 2:11-15

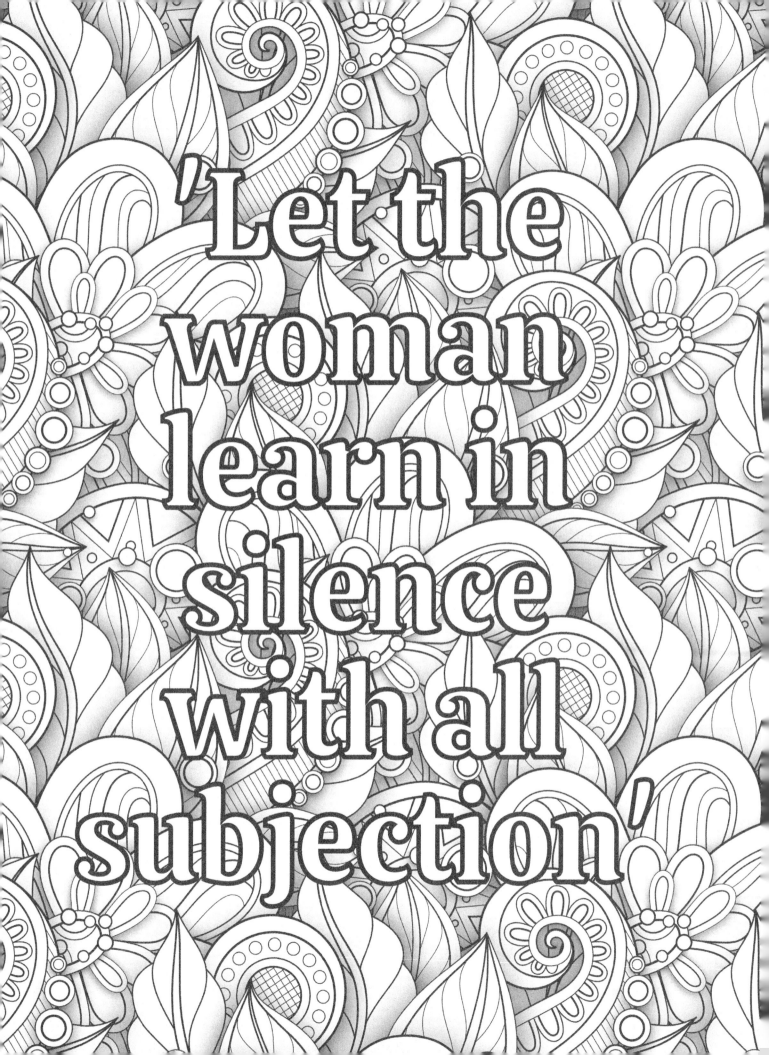

'Be strong and of a good courage, fear not, nor be afraid of them: for the Lord thy God, he it is that doth go with thee; he will not fail thee, nor forsake thee'

Deuteronomy 31:6

'The Lord is my strength and song, and he is become my salvation: he is my God, and I will prepare him an habitation; my father's God, and I will exalt him'

Exodus 15:2

'For the Lord your God is he that goeth with you, to fight for you against your enemies, to save you'

Deuteronomy 20:4

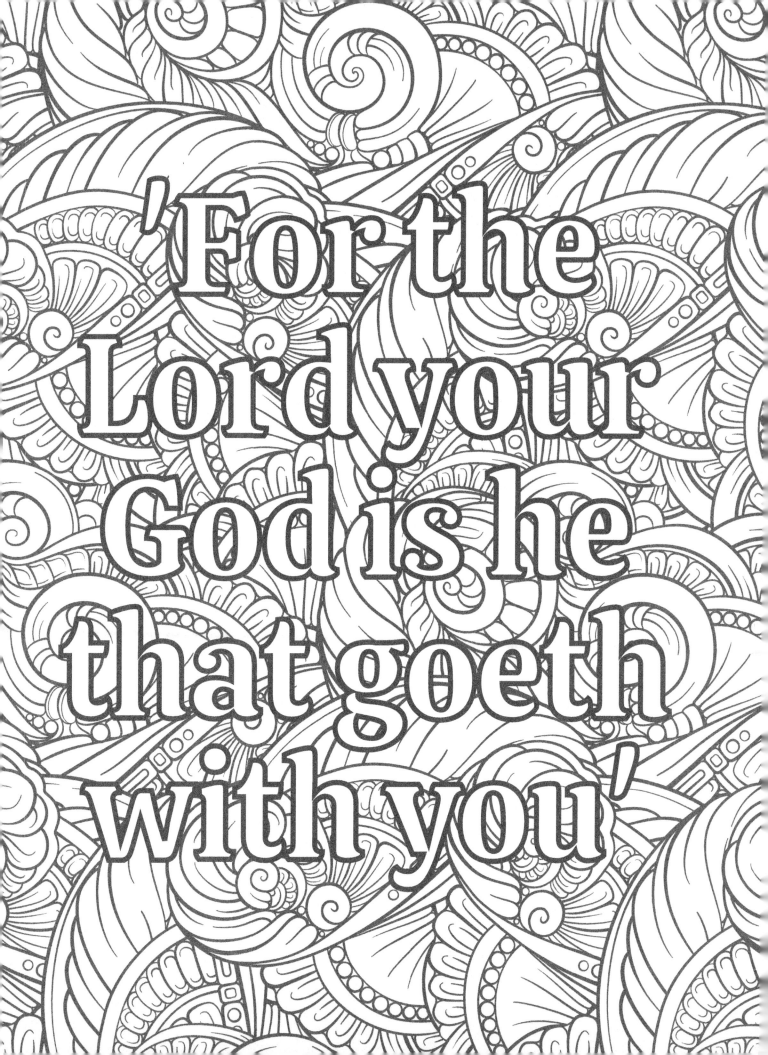

'For the Lord your God is he that goeth with you'

'The Lord is my light and my salvation; whom shall I fear? The Lord is the strength of my life; of whom shall I be afraid?'

Psalms 27:1

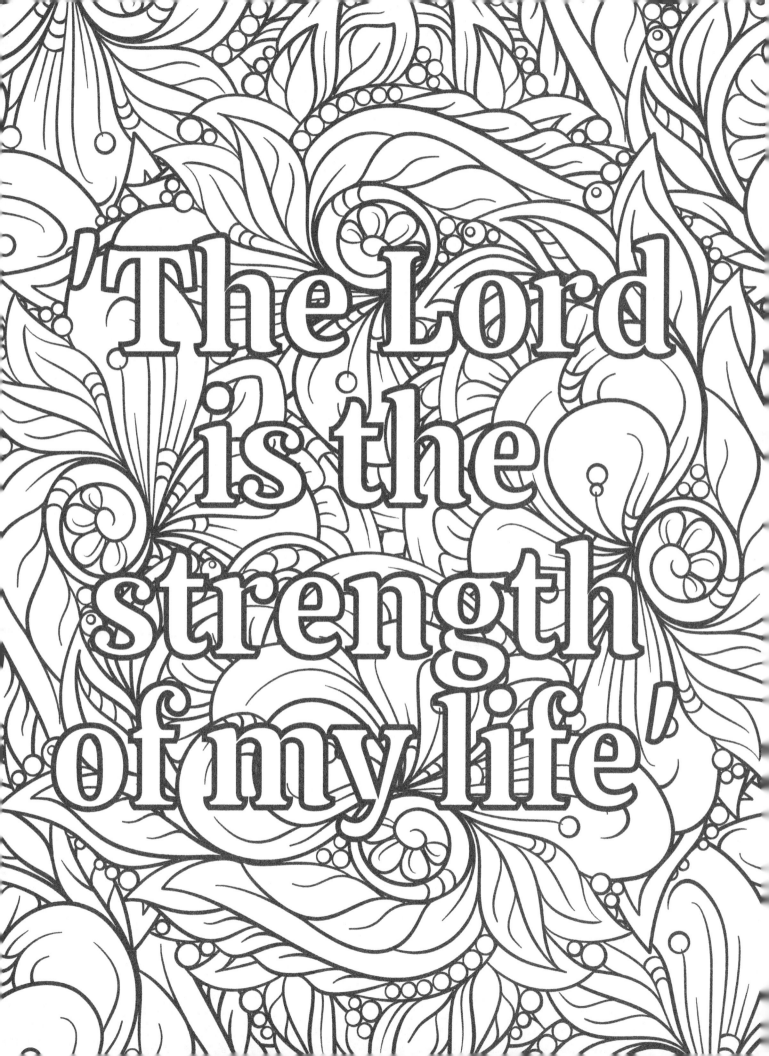

'Be of good courage, and he shall strengthen your heart, all ye that hope in the Lord'

Psalms 31:24

'Be of good courage, and he shall strengthen your heart'

'And thou shalt love the Lord thy God with all thy heart, and with all thy soul, and with all thy mind, and with all thy strength: this is the first commandment'

Mark 12:30

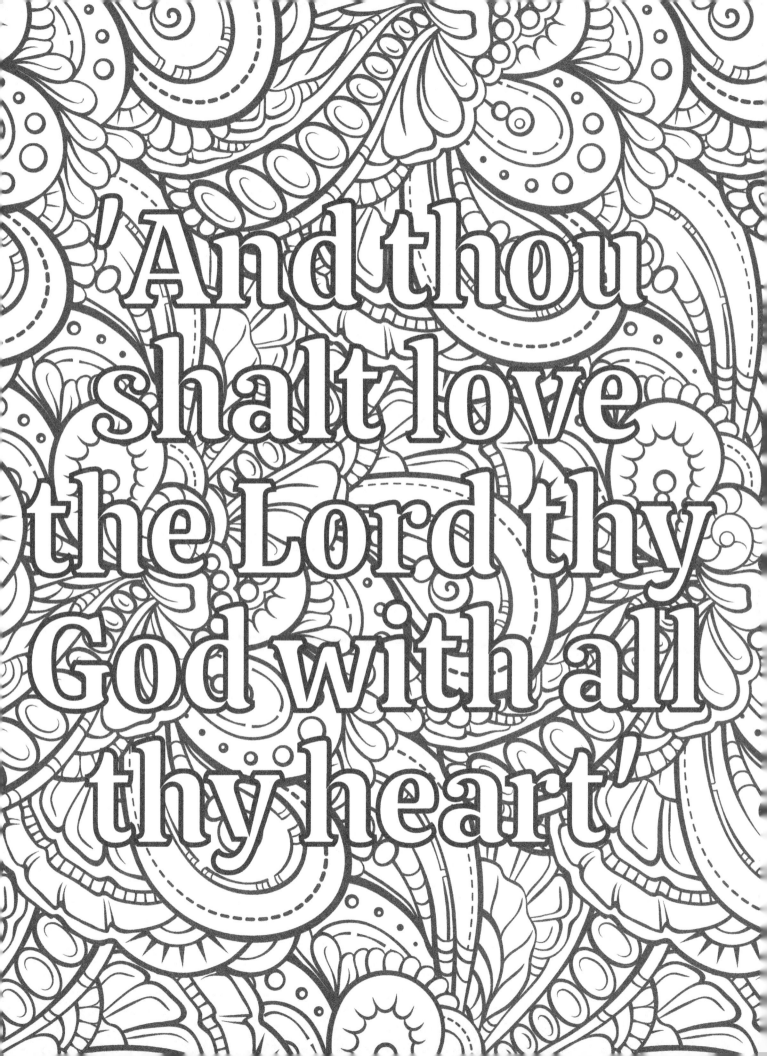

'And thou shalt love the Lord thy God with all thy heart'

'God is our refuge and strength, a very present help in trouble'

Psalms 46:1

'But seek ye first the kingdom of God, and his righteousness; and all these things shall be added unto you'

Matthew 6:33

'Though I walk through the valley of the shadow of death, I will fear no evil: for thou art with me; thy rod and thy staff they comfort me'

Luke 1:45

'For we walk by faith, not by sight'

2 Corinthians 5:7

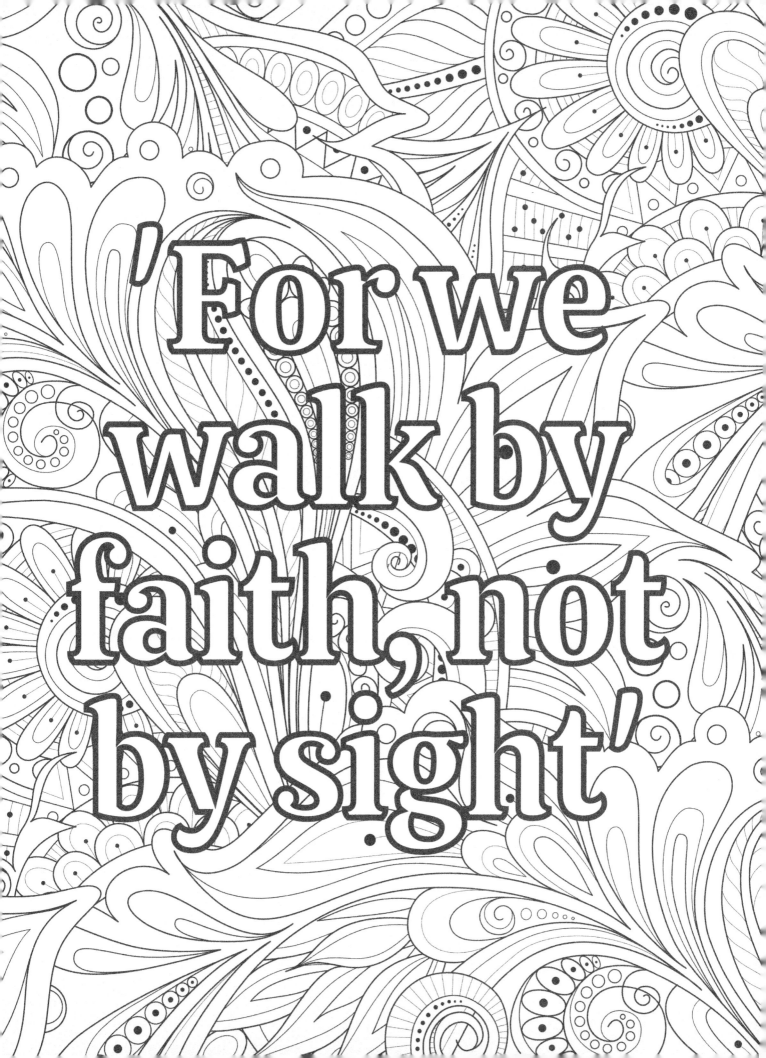

'For with God nothing shall be impossible'

Luke 1:37

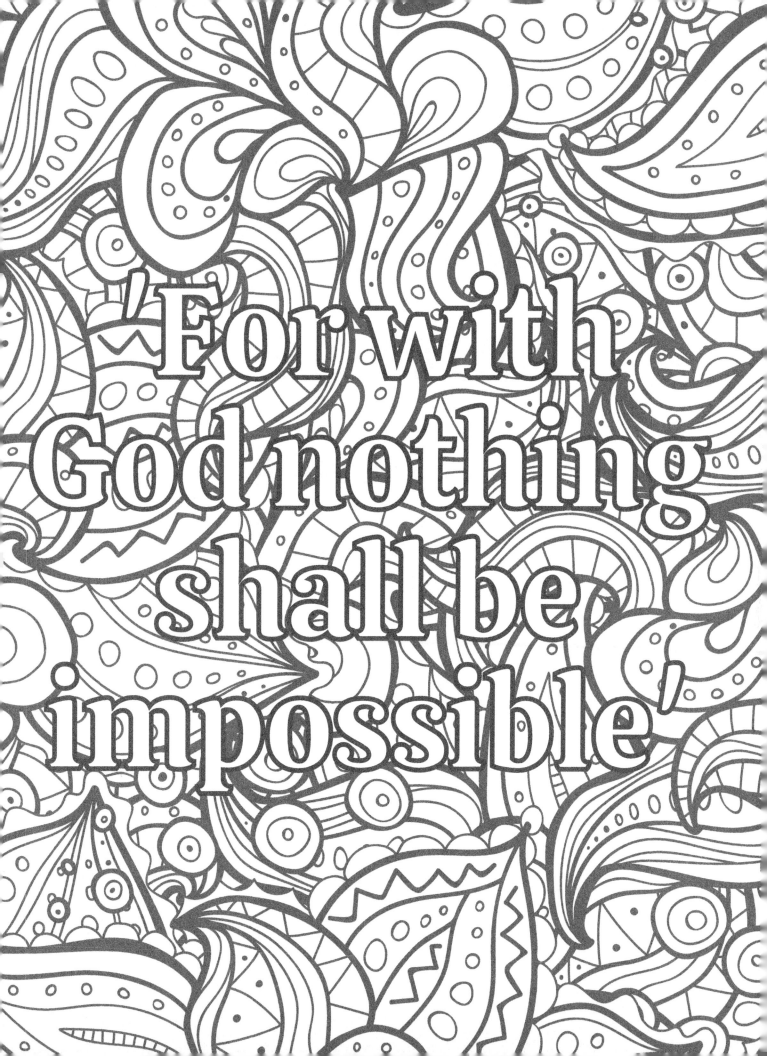

'Be strong.
Be Brave.
Be fearless.
You are
never
alone'

Joshua 1:9

'Therefore, my dear brothers and sisters, stand firm. Let nothing move you'

1 Corinthians 15:58

I hope you will always find
peace, inspiration and
encouragement in
the Good Book.

Leah Nichols

Printed in Great Britain
by Amazon

38829436R00037